We can run

Jenny Giles

Illustrated by Chantal Stewart

"We can run,"
said the children,

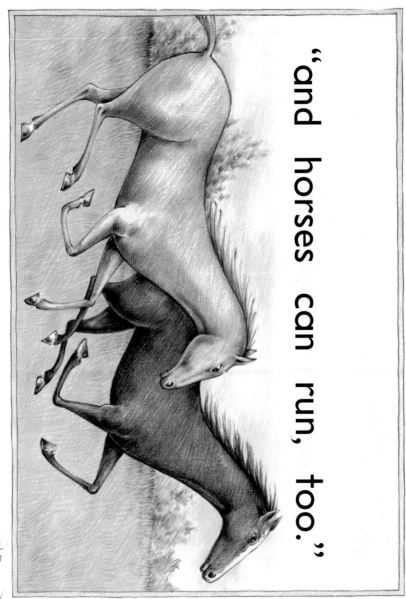

"and horses can run, too."

3

"We can swing," said the children,

"and monkeys can swing, too."

5

"We can crawl," said the children,

6

"and crabs can crawl, too."

"We can jump,"
said the children,

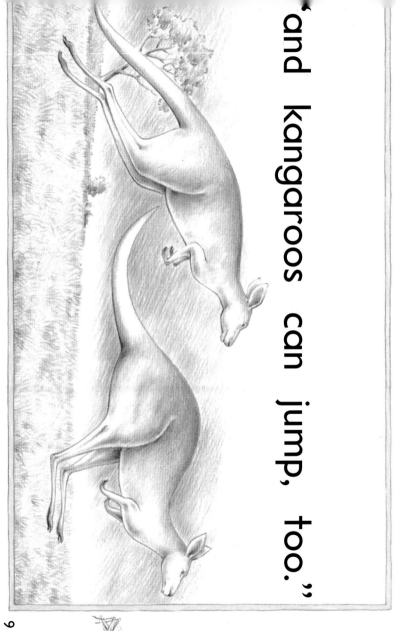

"and kangaroos can jump, too."

"We can climb," said the children,

10

"and cats can climb, too."

"We can swim,"
said the children,

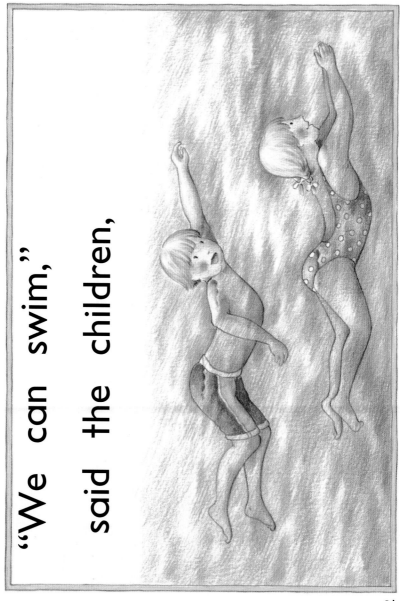

12

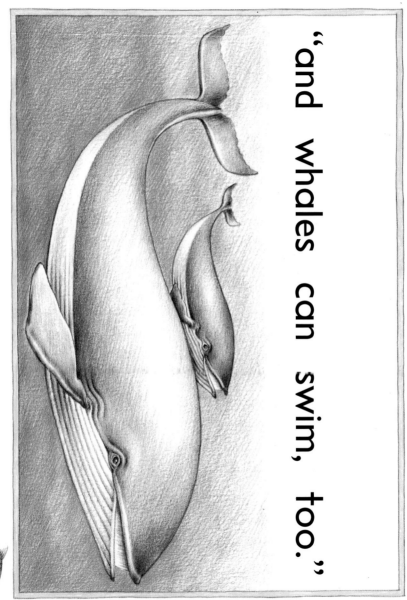

"and whales can swim, too."

"We can dive,"
said the children,

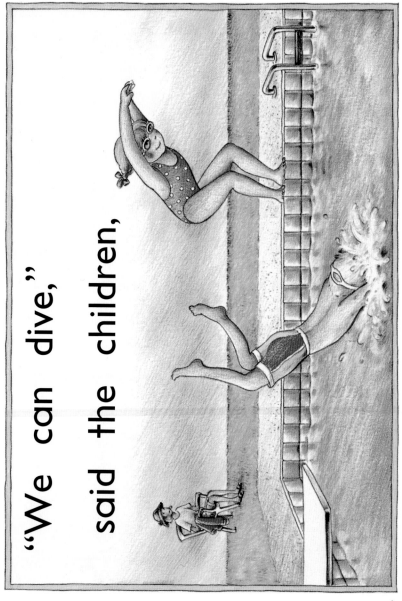

"and penguins can dive, too."

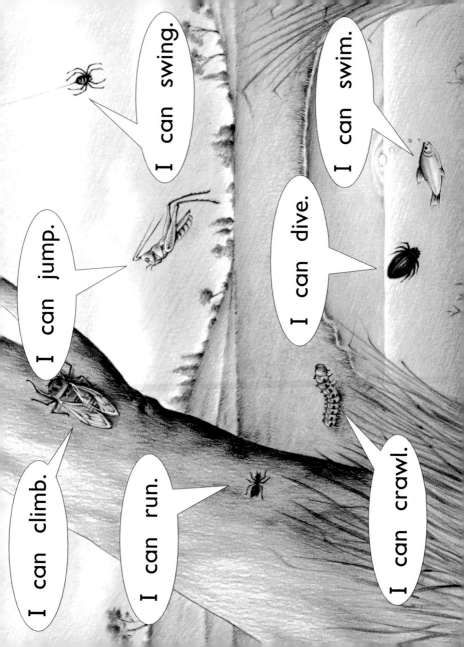